JOHN

JOHN

Rob Wynalda, Joel R. Beeke,
and Paul M. Smalley

REFORMATION HERITAGE BOOKS
Grand Rapids, Michigan

John

Reformation Heritage Books
3070 29th St. SE
Grand Rapids, MI 49512
616-977-0889
orders@heritagebooks.org
www.heritagebooks.org

25 26 27 28 29 30/11 10 9 8 7 6 5 4 3 2

ISBN 979-8-88686-084-9

PREFACE

In Deuteronomy 17, Moses leaves final instructions concerning the future of Israel. As a prophet of God, he foretells that Israel will set a king over the nation (v. 14). This king must be an Israelite, not a foreigner (v. 15), and is forbidden to do certain things (vv. 16–17). In verse 18, Moses transitions to what the king should do. The king is commanded not to simply acquire a copy of the law (the entire book of Deuteronomy), but to handwrite his own copy of the law. The purpose was so that he would read it, fear the Lord, obey, avoid pride, not deviate, and enjoy a long reign (vv. 19–20; cf. Prov. 4:20–27).

More than three thousand years later, modern educators have discovered that students who write out notes by hand have a much higher retention rate than those who simply hear or visually read the information. Apparently, God knew this to be true for the kings of Israel also.

This series of books, known as The Bible Journal, was born from the insight found in Deuteronomy 17:18. Your Bible Journal gives you the opportunity to write out your own copy of a portion of the Holy Scriptures, just as the ancient kings of Israel were instructed to do. Writing out the words of the Bible helps a person to engage the Word of God by slowing down the process of reading the text. Writing answers to the discussion questions also helps you to thoughtfully engage the text. Furthermore, by completing a journal, you leave a legacy to pass on to future generations your insights and personal applications of the text (Deut. 6:6–9; Ps. 78:4–7).

To prepare you to meditate on this portion of the Holy Scriptures, we include an introduction to the book of the Bible to help you understand more thoroughly the Bible book you are about to write out in full. Study Questions and Devotional Reflections have been added after the blank pages set aside for copying each chapter of God's Word. The Study Questions focus on individual verses to keep you thinking about what you are writing, and the Devotional Reflections are designed to help you focus on a few of the major takeaways for your practical Christian life that each Bible chapter provides. We wish to thank Reformation Heritage Books for allowing us to use material drawn from *The Reformation Heritage KJV Study Bible* for the Bible Introduction material and for the Devotional Reflections. The Study Questions have been written by the authors of *The Bible Journal*. Thus, The Bible Journal walks you through a process of getting acquainted with a book of the Bible, copying a chapter by hand, reflecting on the meaning and application of that chapter, and then repeating the process for the next chapter. Families, friends, and small groups can work through a journal together, discussing their meditations for mutual edification as guided by the discussion questions.

The mass production of the Bible since the invention of the printing press has greatly blessed the world. However, there is also great benefit for Bible readers of all ages in following the Deuteronomy 17:18 principle and producing your own handwritten copy of the text.

May God richly bless you in writing and learning His Word through The Bible Journal (Rom. 1:16).

—Rob Wynalda, Joel R. Beeke, and Paul M. Smalley

Introduction to the Book of

JOHN

AUTHORSHIP: The author of this gospel does not identify himself by name but only as "the disciple whom Jesus loved" (21:20, 24). However, there is strong evidence that he was the apostle John, one of the sons of Zebedee. He was an eyewitness of Jesus Christ's life (1:14) and was present at the Last Supper, reclining at the meal beside Jesus (13:23). This identifies him as one of the twelve apostles (Mark 14:17). It may also imply that he was one of the apostles particularly close to Christ, whom the Gospels identify as Peter, James, and John (Mark 5:37; 9:2; 13:3; 14:33). This gospel names other apostles at the Supper, implying that the unnamed disciple was not Thomas, Philip, or the other Judas (John 14:5, 8, 22). Christ chose the beloved disciple to care for His mother, Mary (19:26), another sign that he was especially close to the Lord. He is clearly distinguished from Peter (13:24; 21:20). James, the son of Zebedee, died very early (Acts 12:1–2) and so is unlikely to have written this Gospel. Though it is theoretically possible that one of the lesser known apostles wrote the Gospel, the evidence heavily favors John, the other son of Zebedee, as its author (21:2, 7). This is confirmed by the testimony of later writers, such as Irenaeus (second century AD).

When we refer to the authorship of the books of the Bible we must always remind ourselves that the writers were moved by the Holy Spirit (2 Peter 1:21). God is their ultimate author. So sublime a book as the Gospel of John can only be accounted for as the fruit of divine inspiration. This is how the Bible writers are to be regarded. They were so guided and controlled by God in what they wrote that their writings are to be received by men as infallible and therefore in every way reliable.

DATE: The apostle John died in the last decade of the first century AD. The exact date when he wrote this gospel is not known, but it is probable that he composed it in the last years of his life (AD 90–100).

THEME: Jesus is the Christ, the Son of God, God-in-the-flesh sent by the Father to give eternal life to all whom the Father has given to Him.

PURPOSE: To call people to believe in Christ and so to have eternal life (20:30–31).

SYNOPSIS

The Contribution of John to Redemptive Revelation

We refer to the first three New Testament Gospels as the Synoptic Gospels because they have much in common. (The Greek word *synopsis* means "seeing together"). John's gospel is noticeably different from the other three, though it does not contradict them. It supplements the three Synoptic Gospels and throws wonderful light on the heavenly and glorious person of the Lord Jesus Christ.

Jesus of Nazareth is both God and man (1:1, 14). He showed His glory by His miracles (2:11; 11:39–44) and by His power to rise again from the dead (10:17–18; 20:1–31). He revealed His identity by teaching that He is the Son in a unique relationship with the Father, such that they share one divine essence, power, knowledge, and life (1:18; 5:17–20,26; 10:28–30). He is the Father's eternal Word (1:1), and to see Him is to see the Father (14:9). Therefore Jesus does the works of God, such as judgment and resurrection (5:21–22), and receives worship as God (20:28), not as a rival to the Father but as the One through whom we can know and honor the Father (5:23; 14:9; 17:3).

Jesus used simple illustrations prefaced by the words "I am..." to teach us aspects of His grace and saving power, for example, "I am the light of the world" (8:12). Yet through such simple words He communicated profound truths. The repetition of "I am" (Greek *egō eimi*) at key points in this gospel identifies Christ with *Jehovah* (8:58), the Lord whose name means "I am" (Ex. 3:14). This phrase appears (in the Greek text) on Christ's lips at times when He was demonstrating supernatural power and knowledge (4:26; 6:20; 13:19; 18:5–6). Thus when Jesus used the "I am" phrase to declare that He is the bread of life; the light of the world; the door; the good shepherd; the resurrection and the life; the way, the truth, and the life; and the true vine (6:35; 8:12; 10:7,11; 11:25; 14:6; 15:1), He was declaring that He is the fullness of God come to fill His people in all their needs (4:14; 6:35; 7:37).

With the Father and the Son, the Holy Spirit receives a great deal of attention in this gospel. Jesus spoke of the Spirit as "another Comforter" (14:16), whose ministry would resemble Christ's and continue His work after He had returned to the Father (16:7). Jesus said that the Spirit comes from the Father "in my name" (14:26), not as an independent third party but as One who brings the things the Son received from the Father to the souls of men so that Christ is glorified (16:13–14). The Spirit acts as the Lord and Life-giver (6:63), bringing sinners to a new birth according to the Spirit's sovereign will (3:3–8), so that the wicked become worshipers who exchange worldly lusts for eternal satisfaction in God (4:10,14,23–24; 7:37–39). The Holy Spirit does this work through His Word (6:63), for He is the Spirit of truth (14:17; 15:26; 16:13). He is the witness convicting the world of its guilt (16:8–11) and the guide teaching believers the whole counsel of God (16:13). John gives us a glorious theology of the Trinity that is profoundly relevant for evangelism, worship, and the Christian life.

The triune God appears in John's gospel as a missionary God. John's remarkable teachings about God come in the context not of an abstract theological treatise but as the good news of the divine mission into a perishing world. This appears in John's use of two Greek words, both translated as "send" or "sent" (about sixty times). The Father sent the Son to save perishing sinners out of the world (3:16–17; 6:38–39), and the Spirit anoints and assists Christ in His work (1:32–33; 3:34). The Father and the Son send the Holy Spirit to reveal and glorify the Son (14:26; 15:26; 16:7). The Son also sends His disciples into the world to bear witness to Him by the power of the Spirit (15:26–27; 17:18; 20:21–22). Thus the mission of the church is Trinitarian and God-centered; it comes from God, is performed by God, and aims at God's glory (17:1–5, 10).

Though the book contains many lofty and transcendent teachings, it also portrays Jesus in a most personal way, recording His conversations with a number of individuals. Jesus revealed Himself to an ever-widening group of people: to His early disciples (1:1–51), to the rabbi Nicodemus (3:1–16), to the Samaritan woman (4:1–26), to the man at the Pool of Bethesda (5:1–16), etc. As Christ talked with people, He made it clear that no one has eternal life except those who are born again and so have saving faith in Himself. Formal religion by itself is not pleasing to God. To profess faith without true love for Christ as God's dear Son is worthless in the end. Thus the gospel calls for a personal response to Jesus Christ, as John stated clearly: "But these are written, that ye might believe that Jesus is the Christ, the Son of God; and that believing ye might have life through his name" (20:31).

OUTLINE

I. Christ, the Eternal Son of God (1:1–18)

II. Christ Reveals His Glory in His Public Ministry (1:19–12:50)
   A. Christ's Early Ministry (1:19–4:54)
   B. Christ Rejected by Unbelievers (5:1–6:71)
   C. At the Feast of Tabernacles (7:1–53)
   D. The Woman Taken in Adultery and the Light of the World (8:1–59)
   E. The Healing of the Man Born Blind (9:1–41)
   F. The Good Shepherd (10:1–42)
   G. The Raising of Lazarus (11:1–57)
   H. Conclusion to the Public Ministry (12:1–50)

III. Christ Reveals His Glory in His Passion, Death, and Resurrection (13:1–21:25)
   A. Jesus Washes the Disciples' Feet (13:1–38)
   B. Jesus's Upper Room Discourse and High Priestly Prayer (14:1–17:26)
   C. Jesus's Arrest, Trial, Crucifixion, and Burial (18:1–19:42)
   D. Jesus's Resurrection and Appearances (20:1–21:25)

Notes

Chapter 1

John 1:1–10

1

2

3

4

5

6

7

8

9

10

Notes

John 1:11–17

11

12

13

14

15

16

17

Notes

18

19

20

21

22

23

24

25

Notes

26

27

28

29

30

31

32

Notes

33

34

35

36

37

38

39

Notes

40

41

42

43

44

45

46

Notes

47

48

49

50

51

STUDY QUESTIONS

1. Verse 1: What name is given to Christ here, and what is said about Him?
2. Verse 3: How is Christ related to creation?
3. Verse 7: Why did God send John the Baptist?
4. Verses 10–11: How did most people react when Christ came to earth?
5. Verse 12: How can a person receive Christ? What does Christ give to those who receive Him?
6. Verse 13: What influence has brought them to receive Christ by faith?
7. Verse 14: What does this verse teach about Christ's becoming man?
8. Verse 18: How is it possible to know the invisible God?
9. Verse 23: What prophecy did the ministry of John the Baptist fulfill?
10. Verse 29: What did John say of Christ? What does this mean?
11. Verse 33: What does the descent of the Spirit on Jesus show us about Him?
12. Verses 35–37: How did John's witness about Christ influence some of John's disciples?
13. Verse 41: How is Andrew an example for us of witnessing to people about Christ?
14. Verse 46: Why did Christ's coming from Nazareth not help His reputation?
15. Verse 51: What does Christ's statement to Nathanael mean (see Gen. 28:12–13; Dan. 7:13–14)?

John 1 – Questions and Reflections

DEVOTIONAL REFLECTIONS

1. When John called Jesus "the Word," he implied that Christ not only brings us a message from God but is Himself the Message. Jesus is God in the flesh, the infinite glory and grace of the Father dwelling among men in the tabernacle of a human body. Therefore, to believe in Christ is much more than trusting Him to teach us or help us; saving faith is receiving Him as our God, our very life. What difference does it make to the Christian faith that Christ is God?

2. John the Baptist shows us that a preacher's calling is to point away from himself to Christ and to lift the Savior high before men's eyes. A minister can do this only by having a low view of himself and a high view of Christ. A Christ-centered ministry is particularly a cross-centered ministry, focusing regularly (though not exclusively) on Christ's death as the Lamb of God. How can you pray for ministers that they would be like John in this manner?

3. To find Christ is the most wonderful discovery of all. It is too good to be kept to oneself. How can you become more like these early disciples who eagerly told their family and friends about Jesus?

John 1 – Questions and Reflections

Notes

1

2

3

4

5

6

7

8

9

Notes

John 2:10–16

10

11

12

13

14

15

16

Notes

17

18

19

20

21

22

23

Notes

24

25

STUDY QUESTIONS

1. Verses 1–2: What can you infer about Jesus from His attendance at a wedding feast?
2. Verses 6–9: How much water did Christ make into wine?
3. Verse 10: What was the quality of the wine that Christ made out of water?
4. Verse 11: What was the purpose of Christ's miracle?
5. Verse 15: What did Jesus do in the temple at Jerusalem?
6. Verses 16–17: Why did Jesus do this?
7. Verses 19–21: What did Christ say about His body and what He would do?

DEVOTIONAL REFLECTIONS

1. Miracles performed by Christ are evidences or signs to show us that He is God. The faith of the disciples was strengthened by this first miracle, for it showed that Christ has the power of the Creator over His creation (1:3). The miracle of turning water into wine also suggests the manner in which Christ replaced the rituals of external religion (for which the water pots were used, 2:6) with abundant joy and life. Trusting in Christ means going beyond the outward form of religion and experiencing a new creation within by His power.

2. Carnal men invariably spoil the worship of God in one way or another. Worship must be regulated by God's holy Word. It is a sin to corrupt the public worship in God's house either by commerce or by entertainment. Worship must be reverent. Christ also shows here that discipline is essential to a faithful church. If Christ could cleanse the temple even in His state of humiliation on earth, how much more could He discipline His church as its exalted and glorious Lord? Why should this cause us to conduct worship with holy fear? How can we follow the Lord in His zeal for the purity of God's worship?

John 2 – Questions and Reflections

Notes

1

2

3

4

5

6

7

8

Notes

John 3:9–17

9

10

11

12

13

14

15

16

17

Notes

18

19

20

21

22

23

24

Notes

25

26

27

28

29

30

31

Notes

32

33

34

35

36

STUDY QUESTIONS

1. Verses 3–5: What must happen to a person to see and enter God's kingdom?
2. Verse 8: How does Christ use the wind to illustrate being born of the Spirit?
3. Verse 10: Why did Christ rebuke Nicodemus?
4. Verses 14–15: How did Jesus compare Himself to the bronze serpent (see Num. 21:4–9)?
5. Verse 16: What does this verse teach us about God, Christ, and eternal life?
6. Verses 19–21: Apart from God's grace, how do people respond to Christ? Why?
7. Verses 26–30: How is John a model of humility and love for Christ?
8. Verses 34–35: What does this reveal about the Father, the Son, and the Holy Spirit?
9. Verse 36: How does this verse summarize the two spiritual states of everyone on earth?

John 3 – Questions and Reflections

DEVOTIONAL REFLECTIONS

1. In the church it is not enough for leaders to be academically well trained, nor for its members to be well taught. Without the new birth men are entirely unfit for the kingdom of God. Through the new birth dead sinners are made alive, and at last they will be raised up from the dead to sit with Christ in the glory of heaven. Why is the new birth absolutely necessary for salvation? Are you born again?

2. God's sending of His Son to save the world from condemnation is the greatest display of love in all of human history. God gave His best, His unique Son who shares His very nature, for those who hate and reject Him. Christ was lifted up on the cross to die so that guilty sinners could live forever in relationship with God. What love is this! Why should His love move sinners to trust in Him?

3. We must resist our ignorant and worldly tendency to boast of one minister above another. The abilities and success of each are gifts from heaven. Like John the Baptist, we should have a low view of ourselves and give our full affection and admiration to the Bridegroom. How wonderful is the marriage of the Lord to His people! How can loving Jesus as our spiritual Husband protect us from exalting mere men?

John 3 – Questions and Reflections

Notes

1

2

3

4

5

6

7

8

9

10

Notes

11

12

13

14

15

16

17

Notes

18

19

20

21

22

23

24

25

Notes

26

27

28

29

30

31

32

33

34

Notes

35

36

37

38

39

40

41

Notes

42

43

44

45

46

47

48

49

Notes

50

51

52

53

54

STUDY QUESTIONS

1. Verses 1–2: Who was being baptized? Who was baptizing them?
2. Verse 6: How does this verse show us that Christ is truly human?
3. Verse 9: Why was it surprising for Jesus to speak with this person?
4. Verse 14: What is this water that Christ can give to people? What does it do?
5. Verse 18: Why did Jesus bring up the delicate matter of this woman's husbands?
6. Verse 21: What does the Lord teach about worship here? Why would this be shocking?
7. Verse 24: What does Christ say about God? What does He say about worship?
8. Verses 28–29: What did the Samaritan woman do after talking to Jesus?
9. Verse 34: What does Christ's saying mean? What does it show us about Him?
10. Verses 37–38: How is Christ's statement an antidote to pride in ministry?
11. Verse 42: What did the Samaritans say about Christ? Why?
12. Verses 46–47: Why did this man seek out Jesus?
13. Verses 50–53: How do the distance and timing of this miracle show Christ's power?

John 4 – Questions and Reflections

DEVOTIONAL REFLECTIONS

1. The Christian should learn to turn conversations with unconverted persons to the subject of salvation, as Christ does so kindly here. Christ wisely began with physical, visible things but used them as a lead-in to God's gift and our spiritual need. In our preaching and evangelism we must strive to convince hearers that they have sinned against God. The sinner's conscience is the preacher's friend. However, a sense of sin helps no one without the knowledge of the Savior of the world. Where do you see yourself most in this chapter? The woman confronted, convicted, or converted?

2. Worship is unacceptable to God unless it is "in spirit and in truth" (v. 23). That means that the worshiper must be spiritually reborn and be walking in the Spirit, and that the content and form of worship offered must be according to God's Word. What are some examples of worship that are not done "in spirit"? What are examples of worship not offered "in truth"?

John 4 – Questions and Reflections

Notes

1

2

3

4

5

6

7

8

9

Notes

John 5:10–17

10

11

12

13

14

15

16

17

Notes

18

19

20

21

22

23

Notes

24

25

26

27

28

29

30

Notes

31

32

33

34

35

36

37

Notes

38

39

40

41

42

43

44

45

46

Notes

47

STUDY QUESTIONS

1. Verse 3: Who had gathered in large numbers at the pool called Bethesda?
2. Verse 5: How long had this man been disabled?
3. Verse 8–9: How did Christ heal him? What day was it?
4. Verse 14: What warning did Jesus give the man He healed? What is "a worse thing"?
5. Verse 15: In what sense may it be said that this man betrayed Jesus to His enemies?
6. Verses 16–18: What are two reasons why some Jews sought to kill Christ?
7. Verses 19–20: How many of the Father's works does the Son share in?
8. Verses 22–23: What is the Father's purpose in making His Son the judge?
9. Verses 28–29: What will the Son do by the power of His voice one day?
10. Verse 35: How does Jesus describe John? What does this metaphor mean?
11. Verses 39–40: To whom do the Scriptures testify? Why, then, do many not have eternal life?
12. Verse 44: What's one thing that makes it impossible for people to believe in Christ?
13. Verse 47: If people are going to believe in Christ, what else must they believe?

John 5 – Questions and Reflections

DEVOTIONAL REFLECTIONS

1. Christ blessed the cripple before he had even asked to be healed. Yet He also issued a strong call to repentance (v. 14). Many who receive physical or material blessings from Christ do not acknowledge God in a life of repentance. How have you experienced earthly blessings from Christ? What does it mean for you to hear Christ's "Sin no more, lest a worse thing come unto thee" (v. 14)?

2. None will ever honor Christ rightly until they recognize that He is the eternal Son of God incarnate. From all eternity the Father, the Son, and the Holy Spirit have shared one divine nature, with one will and one power. They cooperate in a beautiful relationship as three persons in one God. Honoring the Son as God does not demean the Father, for honoring the Son is the way through which the Father desires to be honored. How can we honor the Son as the Giver of eternal life? As the Judge?

John 5 – Questions and Reflections

Notes

1

2

3

4

5

6

7

8

9

Notes

10

11

12

13

14

15

16

Notes

17

18

19

20

21

22

23

Notes

24

25

26

27

28

29

30

31

Notes

32

33

34

35

36

37

38

39

Notes

40

41

42

43

44

45

46

47

48

49

Notes

50

51

52

53

54

55

56

57

Notes

58

59

60

61

62

63

64

65

Notes

66

67

68

69

70

71

STUDY QUESTIONS

1. Verses 5–6: Why did Jesus ask Philip how to get food for all those people?
2. Verse 7: How much would it cost to buy food for this crowd?
3. Verses 9–10: How much food did the disciples have to feed five thousand men (and others)?
4. Verse 13: How much food was left over? How does this show the glory of Christ?
5. Verse 15: Why did Jesus go alone to the mountain?
6. Verse 19: What does this miracle show us about Christ?
7. Verses 26–27: How did Christ reprove the people for seeking Him for the wrong reason?
8. Verse 29: What is the work that God requires of us? Why is this so important?
9. Verse 35: What does Christ say of Himself? What does it tell us about Him and faith in Him?
10. Verse 37: What does Jesus teach us about the power of God's grace? About Christ's mercy?
11. Verse 38: What does the Son of God teach us about Himself?
12. Verse 44: What do we need God to do so that we come to Christ?
13. Verse 46: How is the Son greater than all mere men?
14. Verse 51: What does Jesus mean when He says, "The bread that I will give is my flesh"?
15. Verses 53–57: Why must we "eat" Christ? How do we do that (see v. 35)?
16. Verse 63: How is it that God gives life ("quickeneth")?
17. Verses 68–69: Why didn't Simon Peter turn away from Christ?
18. Verse 70: What did Christ know was already true of Judas Iscariot?

John 6 – Questions and Reflections

DEVOTIONAL REFLECTIONS

1. The crowds were attracted by Christ's miracles, but not by His power to save souls. In the same way the "health and wealth" gospel attracts many but does not stress the need for true conversion. Only when men are converted do they put spiritual and heavenly values first in life. When Jesus challenged the crowds, He lost much of His visible following. Why must churches be willing to challenge men's worldliness, even if doing so may reduce their numbers?

2. None can come to Christ for salvation but those whom God Himself draws. The truths of the gospel will always be offensive to those who are unconverted. The preacher is not at liberty to alter the truth in order to gain the favor of unbelieving sinners, as our Lord Himself here shows by His perfect example. Instead, the church must rely on the Spirit of God to do what no man can. How does this call us to fervent and regular prayer for the preaching of the Word?

John 6 – Questions and Reflections

Notes

1

2

3

4

5

6

7

8

9

10

Notes

11

12

13

14

15

16

17

Notes

18

19

20

21

22

23

24

25

Notes

26

27

28

29

30

31

Notes

32

33

34

35

36

37

38

Notes

39

40

41

42

43

44

45

46

Notes

47

48

49

50

51

52

53

STUDY QUESTIONS

1. Verses 3–5: What did Jesus's brothers urge Him to do? Why?
2. Verse 7: Why did the world hate Christ? How might such hatred show itself?
3. Verse 12: How did people view Jesus at this time?
4. Verse 16: From whom did Christ get the doctrine He taught?
5. Verse 17: What must be true of us if we are to discern whether a doctrine is from God?
6. Verses 22–23: How did Jesus argue that healing is lawful on the Sabbath?
7. Verse 24: How should we judge Christ and, indeed, any person?
8. Verse 30: Why couldn't anyone seize Jesus (see John 8:20)? What does this teach us?
9. Verse 34: What did Christ mean by, "Where I am...ye cannot come"?
10. Verses 37–39: What are rivers of living water? Why were they not yet given?
11. Verse 42: Why did some people mistakenly think Jesus was not the Christ?
12. Verses 45–46: Why didn't the officers arrest Jesus at this time?
13. Verse 51: What objection did Nicodemus raise against how they were treating Jesus?

John 7 – Questions and Reflections

DEVOTIONAL REFLECTIONS

1. The unbelief of Jesus's brothers sets forth the important lesson that we can be near the truth and yet lack true faith. It is a mercy that after Christ's resurrection we find Christ's brothers in the company of those who believe. How is their unbelief a warning to those growing up in Christian families and churches? How is their conversion an encouragement with regard to what God can do?

2. Christ still says through the gospel, "If any man thirst, let him come unto me, and drink" (v. 37). He proclaims Himself to all who hear the gospel, promising that everyone who trusts in Him will receive the eternal life of God's Spirit and become a means by which the Spirit overflows to others. Sadly, many people stumble over their pride and so reject Him. Others depend on hearsay about Christ and fail to seek the facts that confirm His Messiahship and deity. How have you responded to Christ's call to come to Him?

John 7 – Questions and Reflections

Notes

1

2

3

4

5

6

7

8

9

Notes

10

11

12

13

14

15

16

17

Notes

18

19

20

21

22

23

24

25

Notes

26

27

28

29

30

31

32

33

34

Notes

35

36

37

38

39

40

41

42

Notes

43

44

45

46

47

48

49

50

Notes

51

52

53

54

55

56

57

58

59

STUDY QUESTIONS

1. Verses 3–4: Who is missing here (see Lev. 20:10)? What does that imply?
2. Verse 7: How did Christ respond to their demand for this woman's death?
3. Verse 11: How do Christ's words express both His grace and His righteousness?
4. Verse 12: What did Jesus say about Himself? What does this mean?
5. Verse 19: What does this saying imply about knowing God?
6. Verse 24: What warning does Christ give to those who do not believe in Him?
7. Verse 29: How does Jesus describe His relationship with the Father?
8. Verses 31–32: What are the mark and the privileges of Christ's true disciples?
9. Verses 34–36: What kind of freedom does God's Son give to people? Do you have it?
10. Verse 39: What is the mark of a true child of Abraham?
11. Verse 44: Who is the spiritual father of unbelievers? What does Christ say about him?
12. Verse 48: How did the unbelieving Jews respond to Christ's teaching?
13. Verse 51: What does this promise mean?
14. Verse 56: What does Jesus say about Abraham?
15. Verse 58: What does Christ say about Himself? What does this imply about Him (see Ex. 3:14)?

John 8 – Questions and Reflections

DEVOTIONAL REFLECTIONS

1. Christ came not to condemn sinners but to save them. The worst of sinners in this life may be saved, if he will repent and trust in Christ. Rather than judging sinners in pride and hypocrisy, we should bring them to Jesus to learn of His grace. The Son is able truly and lastingly to set sinners free!

2. Christ did not hold back from saying hard things to sinners who were not yet broken over their sins. He stripped them of their religious presumption based on their backgrounds and upbringings. He warned them of their slavery to sin and told them they were so bad they were unable to believe in Him. He even said they were children of Satan, the image-bearers of the great murderer and liar. Why did Jesus say such things to religious people who believed in Him? Why did He not speak this way to the woman caught in adultery? Have you submitted to what God says about you?

John 8 – Questions and Reflections

Notes

1

2

3

4

5

6

7

8

Notes

9

10

11

12

13

14

15

16

Notes

17

18

19

20

21

22

23

Notes

24

25

26

27

28

29

30

31

Notes

32

33

34

35

36

37

38

39

40

Notes

41

STUDY QUESTIONS

1. Verse 1: What was the man's problem, and how long had he suffered from it?
2. Verses 2–3: What does the disciples' question assume? How did Jesus correct them?
3. Verse 5: What might this suggest about the spiritual significance of Christ's healing the blind?
4. Verses 8–9: How did this miracle result in some confusion among the man's neighbors?
5. Verse 16: How did this miracle provoke division among the Pharisees?
6. Verses 20–22: What did the man's parents verify? What did they not say? Why not?
7. Verse 25: What did the man know for sure?
8. Verses 30–33: How did the man show himself wiser than the Pharisees?
9. Verses 35–37: What did Jesus later teach the man?
10. Verse 38: How did the man respond?

DEVOTIONAL REFLECTIONS

1. God has given each of His servants a day to work, but the night is coming. Until the Lord returns we will all die. Therefore, let us learn to redeem our time. Even the sorrows of this fallen world are opportunities to glorify God.

2. Christ's Word confronts us, and there is no neutrality. We can be like the man who was healed and boldly follow the truth to worship at the feet of Jesus and confess Him before men; like his parents, who in the fear of man bowed under the intimidation of this world; or like the Pharisees, who were so blind they rejected the plain truth to cling to their own ways. Only one of these individuals or groups could see; the others were blind to the light of Christ's glory. Which do you most resemble?

John 9 – Questions and Reflections

Notes

1

2

3

4

5

6

7

8

Notes

9

10

11

12

13

14

15

Notes

16

17

18

19

20

21

22

23

Notes

24

25

26

27

28

29

30

31

32

33

Notes

34

35

36

37

38

39

40

Notes

41

42

STUDY QUESTIONS

1. Verses 1–2: How do these verses contrast the true Shepherd to false leaders?
2. Verses 3–4: How do the Shepherd and the sheep relate to each other?
3. Verse 9: What does Jesus mean by calling Himself "the door" (see John 14:6)?
4. Verses 14–16: How would you explain Christ's teaching without using the metaphor of sheep?
5. Verses 17–18: What does Jesus teach us about His death?
6. Verses 19–21: How do we again see the division among the Jews concerning Jesus?
7. Verse 27: What is a distinguishing mark of Christ's sheep? Are you one of His sheep?
8. Verses 28–29: What promise does Christ give to His sheep?
9. Verse 30: Why is this saying one reason to believe in the doctrine of the Trinity?
10. Verse 35: What is Christ's view of the Holy Scriptures?
11. Verse 38: What should we learn from Christ's miracles?

John 10 – Questions and Reflections

DEVOTIONAL REFLECTIONS

1. Jesus claimed to be the great Shepherd of God's people. He is the King who loves His people and cares for them intimately and individually. No one is truly a sheep in Christ's flock who does not listen to Him and follow Him. What does this parable teach us about true discipleship to Jesus?

2. While the image of a shepherd is comforting, Jesus used it to call people to follow Him in the midst of thieves, robbers, and fierce wolves. Indeed, Jesus is an unusual Shepherd, for He defends His flock by dying for His sheep. What spiritual dangers did Jesus describe in this parable? How can we find safety from them?

3. God has given to Jesus a particular people, His "sheep," to save and bring to eternal life (vv. 27–29). Christ knows them in a special way (v. 14), for He died for them in particular (vv. 11, 15). They will hear His voice in Scripture and obey Him (vv. 4, 16, 27), and only they will believe in Him (vv. 26). He will never lose them, for the power of God keeps them safe (vv. 28–29). These verses epitomize the doctrines of election, particular redemption, effectual calling, and perseverance of the saints. How do these truths give comfort to believers? How do they encourage evangelism?

John 10 – Questions and Reflections

Notes

1

2

3

4

5

6

7

8

9

Notes

10

11

12

13

14

15

16

17

18

Notes

19

20

21

22

23

24

25

26

27

28

Notes

29

30

31

32

33

34

35
36

37

Notes

38

39

40

41

42

43

44

45

46

Notes

47

48

49

50

51

52

53

Notes

54

55

56

57

STUDY QUESTIONS

1. Verse 4: What was the purpose of Lazarus's sickness?
2. Verses 5–6: Why does verse 5 seem to contradict verse 6? What is happening here?
3. Verse 11: What did Jesus mean by this statement about sleeping and waking?
4. Verses 14–15: How do Christ's words show us His priorities in our lives?
5. Verse 17: How long had Lazarus been in the grave when Jesus arrived?
6. Verse 21: How do Martha's words express her pain and confusion and yet her faith?
7. Verse 24: What did Martha believe about the future?
8. Verse 25: How did Christ bring that future hope into the present and focus it on Himself?
9. Verse 29: How did Mary respond when she heard that Christ called her?
10. Verse 35: What does this show us about Jesus?
11. Verses 41–42: What did Jesus pray? Why?
12. Verses 43–44: How did Christ raise Lazarus from the dead? How does that show His glory?
13. Verses 50–52: What did the high priest prophesy about Christ?
14. Verse 53: How did the chief priests and Pharisees react to Christ's raising Lazarus to life?
15. Verse 54: What did Jesus do in light of their plots against Him?

John 11 – Questions and Reflections

DEVOTIONAL REFLECTIONS

1. Since Christ's death is the death of death to all His people, they need not sorrow excessively when facing death. In the great day the voice of Jesus will raise up all believers in glory. Though believers die physically, they never die spiritually or eternally but will rise at last to meet the Lord in the air at His second coming (1 Thess. 4:13–16). How do these truths affect the way in which you will face death?

2. Though Christ is the infinite and living God, He is also a man with a human mind and emotions like our own. Therefore, we need not fear to approach Him but can pour out our hearts to Him and know He will sympathize with all except those who are rebellious against God. Here is a Priest who can help us in temptation. Consider that "Jesus wept" (v. 35). How does that encourage you to seek Him as the sympathizing High Priest (Heb. 4:15)?

John 11 – Questions and Reflections

Notes

1

2

3

4

5

6

7

8

Notes

9

10

11

12

13

14

15

16

Notes

17

18

19

20

21

22

23

24

Notes

25

26

27

28

29

30

31

Notes

32

33

34

35

36

37

38

Notes

39

40

41

42

43

44

45

46

Notes

47

48

49

50

STUDY QUESTIONS

1. Verse 3: What did Mary do for the Lord Jesus? Why (see v. 7)?
2. Verse 6: Why did Judas criticize Mary for what she did?
3. Verse 9: Why did such large crowds come to see Jesus as Passover drew near (see vv. 17–18)?
4. Verse 13: How did the crowds welcome Jesus into Jerusalem?
5. Verses 14–15: Why did Jesus ride on the colt of a donkey?
6. Verses 20–21: Why was it significant that Greeks sought to see Jesus?
7. Verse 24: What is the meaning of this parable?
8. Verses 27–28: How did Jesus feel about what was coming? Why didn't He try to escape it?
9. Verses 31–33: What were two of the amazing results of Christ's death?
10. Verse 36: How would you explain the meaning of this saying about light?
11. Verses 38–41: What passages from Isaiah's prophecy were fulfilled in Christ? How?
12. Verses 42–43: What hinders some people from confessing Christ openly?
13. Verse 48: On the last day, what will judge the people who rejected Christ?

John 12 – Questions and Reflections

DEVOTIONAL REFLECTIONS

1. Those who love Christ and honor Him must expect to be critically misjudged by those who are only nominal Christians. That should not discourage them from pouring out their lives in love for the One who died for them. How can you imitate Mary's costly devotion?

2. The death of Christ is the most sublime of all God's works to glorify Himself. In His dying, Christ has in a unique way manifested the love, justice, and wisdom of God. At the cross Satan's power was broken and the nations redeemed. The cross of Christ breaks the hearts of all elect sinners and leads them to devote their lives to Him. In what way do you see God's glory in Christ crucified? How does that draw you to Christ as Savior and Lord?

John 12 – Questions and Reflections

Notes

1

2

3

4

5

6

7

8

Notes

9

10

11

12

13

14

15

16

Notes

17

18

19

20

21

22

23

24

25

Notes

26

27

28

29

30

31

32

Notes

33

34

35

36

37

38

STUDY QUESTIONS

1. Verse 1: What did Jesus do when He knew He would soon return to His glory?
2. Verses 4–5: How did Christ show His love? Why was this shocking?
3. Verse 8: What did Jesus mean by, "If I wash thee not, thou hast no part with me"?
4. Verse 10: How are believers already washed and clean? Why do they need regular cleansing?
5. Verse 14: What does it mean "to wash one another's feet"? How can we do that?
6. Verse 18: What was being fulfilled in these events (see Ps. 41:9)?
7. Verse 19: Why did Christ foretell His betrayal? What does this show about Him?
8. Verse 27: Who was working in Judas to move him to betray Christ (see v. 2)?
9. Verse 31: As Christ's sufferings were about to begin, what did He say?
10. Verse 35: How can people know who Jesus's true disciples are?

John 13 – Questions and Reflections

DEVOTIONAL REFLECTIONS

1. As Christ looked beyond the cross to the crown which He was soon to wear, so believers should look beyond their earthly trials to the glory that will be theirs at last. How can this hope empower you to humbly serve others as Christ did?

2. God is in control of every situation. Judas had his covetous eye on the money promised to him, but God's purpose was to save a multitude of sinners through Christ's shed blood. How profound are Peter's words in his sermon on the day of Pentecost: "Him, being delivered by the determinate counsel and foreknowledge of God, ye have taken, and by wicked hands have crucified and slain" (Acts 2:23). If God can even use a traitor to provide salvation, how are you motivated to trust Him with your trials now?

3. A Christian may have much to learn about his own weakness. Mercifully, God is ready to forgive all who have true faith. Peter was a true child of God, yet he fell through overconfidence; Judas was no true child of God but a hypocrite, and he went to his own place. Let every man search his own heart and ask, "Lord, is it I?" (Matt. 26:22).

John 13 – Questions and Reflections

Notes

1

2

3

4

5

6

7

8

Notes

9

10

11

12

13

14

15

16

Notes

17

18

19

20

21

22

23

Notes

24

25

26

27

28

29

30

Notes

31

STUDY QUESTIONS

1. Verse 2: What is one reason Christ ascended to the Father?
2. Verse 6: How is Christ the only way, truth, and life of God?
3. Verse 9: What did Jesus say about the one who has seen Him?
4. Verses 13–14: What did Christ promise about prayer? What does this mean?
5. Verses 16–17: Whom did Christ promise to send? What do His titles mean (see v. 26; John 15:26)?
6. Verse 21: What will we do if we love the Son? What will He do for those who love Him?
7. Verse 23: What will the Father and the Son do for those who love God?
8. Verse 27: What has Christ left for His disciples after He returned to the Father?
9. Verses 30–31: Who was coming for Christ? Why did Christ permit this to happen?

DEVOTIONAL REFLECTIONS

1. Just as Jesus showed His love by washing the feet of His disciples (13:1–17), so He demonstrated His great mercy by teaching them in the upper room just before He was arrested and killed (14:1–16:33). Rather than turning inward as His death approached, Christ devoted Himself all the more to serving others. Rather than demanding comfort, He disbursed it to others. How can we imitate His example?

2. Verse 6 is one of Christ's most loved statements, a precious distillation in just a few words of all that He is for His people. How have you known Christ as your way? Your truth? Your life? Why is He the only way to the Father?

3. As Jesus prepared His disciples for His departure, He repeatedly pointed them to the divine person who would continue Christ's ministry among them after Jesus left: the Holy Spirit. What does this chapter teach us about the Spirit's work and why we need Him?

John 14 – Questions and Reflections

Notes

1

2

3

4

5

6

7

8

Notes

9

10

11

12

13

14

15

16

17

Notes

18

19

20

21

22

23

24

25

Notes

26

27

STUDY QUESTIONS

1. Verse 1: How did Christ describe Himself and the Father? What does this mean?
2. Verses 5–6: What comes from abiding in Christ? What comes from not abiding in Him?
3. Verse 8: What are the ultimate results of abiding in Christ?
4. Verses 12–13: What is Christ's command for us? How is He our great example?
5. Verse 16: What is the ultimate reason why His disciples bear fruit?
6. Verses 18–21: Why does the world hate Christ's disciples?
7. Verse 23: What is true about someone who hates Christ?
8. Verses 26–27: What does the Holy Spirit do as we bear witness for Christ?

DEVOTIONAL REFLECTIONS

1. Jesus is the Vine and Christians are the branches. Without the Lord we can do nothing pleasing to the Lord. Union and communion with Christ are crucial to a fruitful spiritual life that pleases God. By rejecting Christ the unbelieving Jews cut themselves off from their only hope of becoming what God intended Israel to be. Jews and Gentiles who trust in Christ become God's true vineyard. Do you abide in Christ by a living faith? What fruits are you bearing that demonstrate this? How can you cultivate a deeper life of abiding in the Vine?

2. The history of Christianity illustrates clearly the principle that Christians should expect persecution. Why does the world hate Christ? Why does it hate the servants of Christ? In what way does this teach us our need for the Holy Spirit in order to be effective witnesses for Christ?

John 15 – Questions and Reflections

Notes

1

2

3

4

5

6

7

8

Notes

9

10

11

12

13

14

15

16

17

Notes

18

19

20

21

22

23

24

Notes

25

26

27

28

29

30

31

32

Notes

33

STUDY QUESTIONS

1. Verses 2–3: What did Jewish persecutors of Christians think? Why did they do these things?
2. Verse 7: Why is it better that Christ left us and ascended into heaven?
3. Verses 8–11: What is the Holy Spirit doing in the world?
4. Verse 13: What work does the Holy Spirit do in Christians?
5. Verse 14: How does the Holy Spirit relate to the Son?
6. Verses 18–19: What were the disciples confused about?
7. Verses 23–24: What promise does Jesus give? What does "in my name" mean?
8. Verse 28: Where did Christ come from? What was His destination?
9. Verse 32: How was Jesus alone? How was He not alone?
10. Verse 33: Why did Christ say these things? What encouragement does He give to us?

John 16 – Questions and Reflections

DEVOTIONAL REFLECTIONS

1. Not only are men and women perishing in their sins under the wrath of God and unable and unwilling to come to Christ, but they are strangely unaware of their desperate condition. The Spirit must awaken them to their guilt before God; the perfection of the Savior, Jesus Christ; and the reality that God's judgment on this wicked world has already begun in Christ's victory over Satan (vv. 7–11). How should this truth motivate and guide us in praying for the Spirit's help in our evangelism?

2. The Spirit is the Teacher of the church, bringing to us the glories of Christ so that we may see that all the fullness of the Father is in Christ for our benefit (vv. 12–15). How often do you pray for the work of the Spirit in the church of Christ? How can you be more fervent in your prayers for the Holy Spirit?

3. The Christian's life is a strange paradox in this world, a puzzling mixture of distress and peace, fear and courage (vv. 32–33). Why is this so? How can we grow in peace and courage by pleading the promise "I have overcome the world"?

John 16 – Questions and Reflections

Notes

1

2

3

4

5

6

7

8

Notes

9

10

11

12

13

14

15

16

Notes

John 17:17–24

17

18

19

20

21

22

23

24

Notes

25

26

STUDY QUESTIONS

1. Verse 2: What does this say about Christ's position and mission?
2. Verse 3: What is eternal life?
3. Verse 5: What does this say about the glory Christ entered when He ascended into heaven?
4. Verse 9: For whom did Christ pray? What does this imply about His intercession in heaven?
5. Verse 15: What did Jesus not ask the Father? What did He ask?
6. Verse 21: What is Christ's prayer for believers? What is His goal in this?
7. Verse 24: What is Christ's ultimate desire for His people? Why has the Father glorified Him?

DEVOTIONAL REFLECTIONS

1. This great, high-priestly prayer of Christ is the consummation of the preceding discourse (14:1–16:33). We see here a sample of the intercessory work of Christ at the right hand of God. Everything Christ prays for will be granted by the heavenly Father, since Christ is the God-man whose redemptive work so greatly glorifies God. How can it encourage believers to know that Jesus is interceding with God to preserve them, unify them, and bring them to glory?

2. Christ's prayer for unity (v. 21) has often been used as an argument for church union irrespective of doctrine and practices. However, we must seek unity in a way that honors His prayer, "Sanctify them through thy truth: thy word is truth" (v. 17). There is no true unity without a common faith in the teachings of the inerrant Bible, along with a common life of holiness. Why are these necessary for spiritual unity?

3. The desire of Christ is that Christians will be with Him to gaze upon His glory forever (v. 24). "Blessed are the pure in heart: for they shall see God" (Matt. 5:8). Is this truly your desire? If so, reflect on the truth that heaven is a world of love.

John 17 – Questions and Reflections

Notes

1

2

3

4

5

6

7

Notes

8

9

10

11

12

13

14

15

Notes

16

17

18

19

20

21

22

Notes

23

24

25

26

27

28

29

Notes

30

31

32

33

34

35

36

Notes

37

38

39

40

STUDY QUESTIONS

1. Verse 2: How did Judas know where to find Jesus so that he could betray Him?
2. Verses 5–6: How did the men react when Jesus said, literally, "I am"? Why?
3. Verse 11: Why did Christ command Peter to put away his sword?
4. Verses 15–16: How did Peter and John ("another disciple") get into the high priest's palace?
5. Verses 20–21: How did Jesus respond when questioned about His teachings?
6. Verse 23: How did Christ object against how unfairly they treated Him?
7. Verse 27: What did Peter do that fulfilled Christ's prophecy (see John 13:38)?
8. Verse 31: How did Pilate at first respond to the Jewish leaders' request that Jesus be punished?
9. Verses 36–37: What does Jesus teach here about His kingdom?
10. Verse 38: What was Pilate's view of truth?

DEVOTIONAL REFLECTIONS

1. Christ, as the great "I am," could easily have destroyed His enemies by His divine power (v. 6). He had many powerful servants (the angels) who could have protected Him, but He did not come to be that kind of king (v. 36). Instead, His kingdom comes by preaching and believing the truth (v. 37). What does this teach us about the manner in which the church overcomes this world?

2. Christ was condemned to die under charges of criminal acts (v. 33; 19:12), and the one guilty of criminal acts was set free (18:40). This teaches us two lessons, for both human sin and divine providence were at work here. First, so deep is the hatred and hardness of the hearts of fallen men that they prefer a murderer to the righteous Son of God (Acts 3:14). Second, so deep is the love of God that He sent His Son to die for the sins of His people in order that they, the guilty, would go free (John 3:16–17). How should these truths humble us and fill us with gratitude?

John 18 – Questions and Reflections

Notes

1

2

3

4

5

6

7

8

9

Notes

10

11

12

13

14

15

Notes

16

17

18

19

20

21

22

23

Notes

24

25

26

27

28

29

Notes

30

31

32

33

34

35

36

Notes

37

38

39

40

41

42

STUDY QUESTIONS

1. Verse 2: How do thorns remind us of the judgment due to sin (see Gen. 3:17–18)?
2. Verses 6–7: Why did the chief priests and those with them say that Jesus must die?
3. Verse 11: What did Christ say about Pilate's authority? What does that imply about rulers?
4. Verse 15: What did the priests say about their king? What does this imply about them?
5. Verses 19–20: What was written and posted above Jesus? In what languages was it written?
6. Verse 24: What Scripture was fulfilled by the soldiers who crucified Christ?
7. Verses 26–27: What was Jesus doing in committing His mother and John to each other? Why?
8. Verse 30: What did Christ say before He died? What does it mean?
9. Verses 33, 36: How did the treatment of Christ's body fulfill the Old Testament (see Ex. 12:46)?
10. Verses 38–42: Who buried the body of Jesus? What does this show about them?

John 19 – Questions and Reflections

DEVOTIONAL REFLECTIONS

1. Pontius Pilate will forever be remembered for the gross miscarriage of justice he permitted in the murder of God's Son. We should never allow ourselves to be bullied into doing what in conscience we know to be wrong. Why is the fear of man so powerful as to move people to go against their conscience? How can it be overcome?

2. How clear it is from Christ's willingness to voluntarily undergo such horrible sufferings that He loved His Heavenly Father and also His own dear people! Even as He was dying He was caring for others, as His words to His mother show. Yet His last words, "It is finished" (v. 30), declare that He did not die as a helpless martyr but as the conquering King, even as the sign on the cross stated. In one sense the cross was the chariot on which the King of grace rode to victory over all that had been oppressing His own. Yet He conquered as the Lamb of God, suffering and dying to turn away God's just judgment against sinners. Why should this chapter move us to trust, love, admire, and surrender to this King of infinite grace? How does this chapter affect you?

John 19 – Questions and Reflections

Notes

1

2

3

4

5

6

7

8

Notes

9

10

11

12

13

14

15

16

Notes

17

18

19

20

21

22

23

Notes

24

25

26

27

28

29

Notes

30

31

STUDY QUESTIONS

1. Verses 1–2: Who first brought news to the apostles that Christ's tomb was empty?
2. Verses 6–7: What did Peter find in the tomb?
3. Verse 9: What did the disciples not yet understand?
4. Verse 12: Who appeared to Mary at the tomb?
5. Verse 17: What message did Jesus send to His disciples? What does this imply about them?
6. Verses 19–20: When and where did Christ appear to the disciples?
7. Verse 22–23: How did these words commission the apostles for their future ministry?
8. Verse 27: What proof did Jesus offer to Thomas that He had risen from the dead?
9. Verse 28: What did Thomas call Jesus? What does this reveal about Christ?
10. Verse 31: Why did John write this book? Have you responded to the gospel in this way?

John 20 – Questions and Reflections

DEVOTIONAL REFLECTIONS

1. It is absurd to argue that the resurrection of Christ was a fabrication of the disciples. They were all inclined not to believe it until compelled by the evidence of the risen Jesus. These apostles of Christ have not given us myths or legends but solid, historically reliable accounts of our Lord. Our wisdom is to believe them and to build our lives upon them. What difference would it make to you if Jesus had never risen from the dead? What does that say about your faith?

2. The resurrection appearances of Jesus pulsate with love between Him and His disciples. We see it in the rush of Peter and John to the empty tomb and in the tears of Mary Magdalene. We feel it in the pathos of Jesus's simple address to her—"Mary"—and in her devoted response—"Master." We hear it as Jesus called those who had abandoned Him "my brethren," and reminded them that God is "your Father." He appeared to them with "Peace" on His lips and gently condescended to meet Thomas in his skepticism. Thomas cried out with adoration to the Savior, "My Lord and my God." Do you know the love of the living Lord Jesus? If so, how has His love created in you an answering love for Him?

John 20 – Questions and Reflections

Notes

1

2

3

4

5

6

Notes

7

8

9

10

11

12

13

Notes

14

15

16

17

18

Notes

19

20

21

22

23

24

Notes

25

STUDY QUESTIONS

1. Verses 3–6: When did something like this happen before (see Luke 5:1–11)? What does it mean?
2. Verse 11: What is amazing about the fish? About the net?
3. Verse 15: What question and command did Christ speak to Peter?
4. Verse 17: Why might Christ have said this three times to Peter (see 13:38)?
5. Verses 18–19: What did Jesus foretell about Peter's death?
6. Verse 22: How is this a warning against comparing our lives and ministries to others?
7. Verse 25: How did John end his gospel? How can that statement be true (see John 1:1–3)?

DEVOTIONAL REFLECTIONS

1. The miracle of catching 153 fish, like the feeding of the five thousand, is a sign of Christ's all-sufficient power to enable the apostles (and other gospel preachers) to experience great success as fishers of men (Mark 1:17; Luke 5:10). Yet their fishing all night and catching nothing reminds us that success is not from the preacher or on his terms but subject to Christ's sovereignty. Each servant of God has a future determined by the will of Christ, in some cases a life ending in martyrdom. However, our calling is not to guess about the future but to devote ourselves to following Him by faith. What lessons are there here to encourage you to serve the Lord?

2. Peter's restoration plays a vital role in the conclusion to this gospel because the risen Christ would soon ascend (20:17), having delegated the visible leadership of His people to the apostles and the elders of each church. The apostle Peter was a man broken over his sins against Christ, motivated by his love for Christ, and called to shepherd the people of Christ. Why are all these qualities essential for a minister of the gospel of Jesus Christ?

John 21 – Questions and Reflections